SHEPHERD'S NOTES

SHEPHERD'S NOTES

When you need a guide through the Scriptures

1,2 Peter/Jude

BROADMAN
&HOLMAN
PUBLISHERS

Nashville, Tennessee

© 1998

by Broadman & Holman Publishers

Nashville, Tennessee

All rights reserved

Printed in the United States of America

0–8054–9019–1

Dewey Decimal Classification: 227.92

Subject Heading: BIBLE. N.T. PETER

Library of Congress Card Catalog Number: 97–45195

Library of Congress Cataloging-in-Publication Data

1, 2 Peter, Jude / Dana Gould, editor

      p. cm. — (Shepherd's notes)

    Includes bibliographical references.

    ISBN 0–8054–9019–1

    1. Bible. N.T. Peter, 1st—Study and teaching. 2. Bible. N.T. Peter,
2nd—Study and teaching. 3. Bible N.T. Jude—Study and teaching.
I. Gould, Dana, 1951–.   Series
BS2795.5.A13   1998
222'.9207—dc21

                                    97–45195

                                       CIP

1 2 3 4 5 6   03 02 01 00 99 98

CONTENTS

Dear Reader:

Shepherd's Notes are designed to give you a quick, step-by-step overview of every book of the Bible. They are not meant to be substitutes for the biblical text; rather, they are study guides intended to help you explore the wisdom of Scripture in personal or group study and to apply that wisdom successfully in your own life.

Shepherd's Notes guide you through the main themes of each book of the Bible and illuminate fascinating details through appropriate commentary and reference notes. Historical and cultural background information brings the Bible into sharper focus.

Six different icons, used throughout the series, call your attention to historical-cultural information, Old Testament and New Testament references, word pictures, unit summaries, and personal application for everyday life.

Whether you are a novice or a veteran at Bible study, I believe you will find *Shepherd's Notes* a resource that will take you to a new level in your mining and applying the riches of Scripture.

In Him,

David R. Shepherd
Editor-in-Chief

HOW TO USE THIS BOOK

DESIGNED FOR THE BUSY USER

Shepherd's Notes for 1, 2 Peter, Jude is designed to provide an easy-to-use tool for getting a quick handle on these Bible books' important features, and for gaining an understanding of the message of 1, 2 Peter, Jude. Information available in more difficult-to-use reference works has been incorporated into the *Shepherd's Notes* format. This brings you the benefits of many more advanced and expensive works packed into one small volume.

Shepherd's Notes are for laymen, pastors, teachers, small-group leaders, and participants, as well as the classroom student. Enrich your personal study or quiet time. Shorten your class or small-group preparation time as you gain valuable insights in the truths of God's Word that you can pass along to your students or group members.

DESIGNED FOR QUICK ACCESS

Those with time restraints will especially appreciate the timesaving features built in the *Shepherd's Notes*. All features are intended to aid a quick and concise encounter with the crux of the message.

Concise Commentary. Short sections provide quick "snapshots" of sections, highlighting important points and other information.

Outlined Text. A comprehensive outline covers the entire text of 1, 2 Peter, Jude. This is a valuable feature for following the narrative's flow, and allows for a quick, easy way to locate a particular passage.

Shepherd's Notes. These summary statements appear at the close of every key section of the narrative. While functioning in part as a quick summary, they also deliver the essence of the message presented in the sections they cover.

Icons. Various icons in the margin highlight recurring themes in 1, 2 Peter, Jude and aid in selective searching or tracing of those themes.

Sidebars and Charts. These specially selected features provide additional background information to your study or preparation. These include definitions as well as cultural, historical, and biblical insights.

Maps. These are placed at appropriate places in the book to aid your understanding and study of a text or passage.

Questions to Guide Your Study. These thought-provoking questions and discussion starters are designed to encourage interaction with the truth and principles of God's Word.

In addition to the above features, study aids have been included at the back of the book for those readers who require or desire more information and resources for working through the letters 1, 2 Peter, Jude. These include chapter outlines for studying 1, 2 Peter, Jude and a list reference sources used for this volume, which offer many works that allow readers to extend the scope of their study of these letters.

DESIGNED TO WORK FOR YOU

Personal Study. Using the *Shepherd's Notes* with a passage of Scripture can enlighten your study and take it to a new level. At your fingertips is information that would require searching several volumes to find. In addition, many points of application occur throughout the volume, contributing to personal growth.

Teaching. Outlines frame the text of 1, 2 Peter, Jude and provide a logical presentation of the message. Capsule Thoughts provide summary statements for presenting the essence of key points and events. Personal Application icons point out personal application of the message of 1, 2 Peter, Jude, and Historical Context icons indicate where background information is supplied.

Group Study. Shepherd's Notes can be an excellent companion volume to use for gaining a quick but accurate understanding of the message of a Bible book. Each group member can benefit by having his or her own copy. The *Note's* format accommodates the study of or the tracing of the themes throughout 1, 2 Peter, Jude. Leaders may use its flexible features to prepare for group sessions or use them during group sessions. Guiding Questions can spark discussion of the key points and truths of 1, 2 Peter, Jude.

LIST OF MARGIN ICONS USED IN 1, 2 PETER, JUDE

Shepherd's Notes. Placed at the end of each section, a capsule statement provides the reader with the essence of the message of that section.

Old Testament Reference. To indicate a prophecy fulfillment and its discussion in the text.

New Testament Reference. To indicate New Testament passages that are related to or have a bearing on the passage's understanding or interpretation.

Historical Context. To indicate historical information—historical, biographical, cultural—and provide insight on the understanding or interpretation of a passage.

Personal Application. To indicate a personal or universal application of truth provided in the text.

Word Picture. To indicate that the meaning of a specific word or phrase is illustrated so as to shed light on it.

First Peter provides a message of encouragement for Christians in northern Asia Minor who were facing unbelievable opposition and persecution. Martin Luther named 1 Peter, along with the Gospel of John, 1 John, Romans, Galatians, and Ephesians, as one of the New Testament books that shows us Christ and teaches how Christians ought to live in the world.

1 Peter in a "Nutshell"

Purpose:	To provide encouragement in Christian living.
Major Doctrine:	The sufficiency of God's grace.
Other Key Doctrines:	The return of Christ; the sufferings and sacrifice of Christ on the cross; godly living.

AUTHOR
First Peter begins with an affirmation of Simon Peter's authorship of the letter. Other claims made in the letter support that affirmation. In addition, leaders of the church made frequent references to 1 Peter, and there is no evidence of any dispute about authorship at that time. Only in the twentieth century have some students of 1 Peter questioned whether the apostle wrote the letter.

PURPOSE FOR WRITING
Peter urged his readers to live in accordance with the hope they had received in Christ (1:3). He gave guidance for them to use in their relationships with one another (3:1–12), and he urged them to endure suffering joyfully for Jesus' sake (4:19). His chief aim in writing was to provide them encouragement in Christian living.

DATE AND PLACE OF WRITING

Date. The theme of suffering appears in every chapter of 1 Peter. During Nero's reign there was great persecution of believers. Therefore, the most likely time for the writing of 1 Peter is around A.D. 62–64.

Place. Peter identified Babylon as the place from which he wrote his letter (5:13). Old Testament Babylon in Mesopotamia was deserted during this period. Most likely, he was using the name symbolically to refer to the arrogant idolatry and lust for power that characterized biblical Babylon. He probably used the term as a cryptic designation for Rome.

AUDIENCE

The readers of the letter are identified in 1:1. They lived in the area of Asia Minor north of the Taurus mountains. This was far off the beaten path of travel and commerce. The Bible does not record how the gospel reached this area. Although the area contained colonies of Jews, Gentiles were numerically predominant.

The order in which the provinces are mentioned might suggest the route followed by the letter carrier. He could have landed in Pontus, followed a circuit through the provinces, and left the area at Bithynia.

Although the term *strangers* is the Jewish term for those dispersed from the homeland of Palestine (1:1), Peter probably used it to refer to the church. Peter saw believers as a pilgrim people on earth who had been set apart by God to do His will.

LITERARY FORM

Students of 1 Peter have discussed widely the literary forms within the book. Many find extensive evidence of the presence of hymns, creeds, or fragments of sermons in such passages as 2:4–8 and 2:21–25.

Although these discussions are enlightening and enriching, they are often inconclusive and unconvincing. Peter may have used material from different sources in writing the letter, but it is best to see that he made it his own material under the leadership of the Holy Spirit.

Peter made frequent reference to the Old Testament, sometimes by quotation (2:6–8) and sometimes by allusion (3:6, 20). This frequent use suggests that Jewish readers were at least among the recipients of the letter. Some of Peter's emphases resemble those of Paul. For example, there is similarity between Peter's words about relationships between wives and husbands in 3:1–7 and Paul's discussion in Ephesians 5:22–33.

FIRST PETER AND THE BOOK OF ACTS

Several themes in 1 Peter also appear in the speeches attributed to Peter in Acts, as shown in the following chart.

*Common Themes in 1 Peter and Acts**

THEME	IN ACTS	IN 1 PETER
God is no respecter of persons.	10:34	1:17
Christ is identified as a stone rejected by the builders.	4:10–11	2:7–8
The "name" of Christ has a prominent place.	3:6, 16; 4:10, 12; 5:41	4:14, 16

*(Information taken from Thomas D. Lea, *The New Testament: Its Background and Message*, 534.)

FIRST PETER AND THE GOSPELS

First Peter also contains information we can link to the Gospels. We would expect this to be the case with a letter written by one of the three disciples of the "inner circle."

Common Themes
in 1 Peter and the Gospel of John*

THEME	IN JOHN	IN 1 PETER
Jesus' conversation with Peter	21:1–25	5:2–4
Jesus as the "Chief Shepherd"	10:14	5:4
Being clothed with humility	13:2–17	5:5

*(Information taken from Thomas D. Lea, *The New Testament: Its Background and Message*, 534.)

Some view the entire writing as a sermon preached at the baptism of a group of Christians, viewing the opening section through 4:11 as a message spoken to candidates for baptism. They locate the actual baptism at 1:21–22 and feel that the "Amen" at 4:11 concludes the address to the candidates. The concluding section beginning with 4:12 is viewed as an address to the entire church gathered for the rite of baptism.

THE THEOLOGY OF 1 PETER

Peter often used theological ideas to drive home his ethical demands. He presented the death of Christ as a stimulus for Christians to endure suffering (2:21–25). He also affirmed the resurrection as a chief source of Christian hope and confidence (1:3). He presented the return of Christ as an incentive for holy living (1:13). He portrayed the nature of the Christian call (2:9–10) as a basis for individual Christians to obey Christ at home (3:1–7), to obey Him as servants (2:18–20), and to follow Him as citizens (2:13–17).

BASIC OUTLINE FOR 1 PETER

I. Greetings (1:1–2)
II. The Method and Nature of Salvation
(1:3–12)
III. A Demand for Holiness (1:2–2:3)
IV. A Description of the People of God
(2:4–10)
V. The Christian Witness in the World
(2:11–3:12)
VI. Appeals and Promises to the Persecuted
(3:13–4:19)
V. Praises to God and Greetings to the Church
(5:10–14)

QUESTIONS TO GUIDE YOUR STUDY

1. What was Peter's purpose for writing this letter?
2. Who was his audience? Where were they located?
3. When was 1 Peter written? Why is this dating of the letter significant?
4. How does 1 Peter relate to other portions of the New Testament?

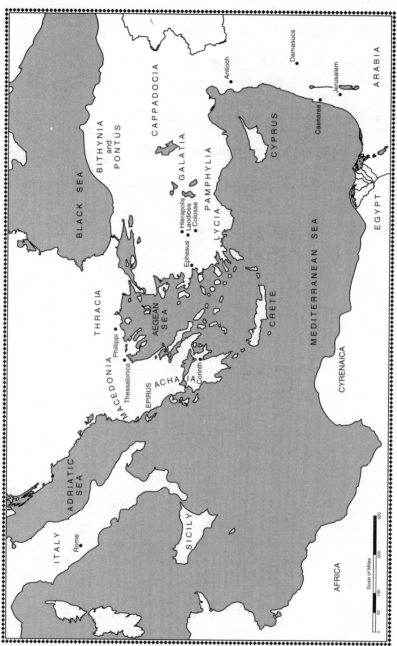

Taken from Richard R. Melick, *Philippians, Colossians, Philemon*, vol. 32, New American Commentary (Nashville, Tenn.: Broadman & Holman Publishers, 1992), p. 37.

SALUTATION (1:1–2)

Author (v. 1)

The author of this book identified himself as "Peter, an apostle of Jesus Christ" (v. 1). *Apostles* were disciples of Jesus called of God and responsible for carrying out God's work in the world.

Peter is credited with being the leader of the original Twelve Disciples whom Jesus called. As a member of the inner circle, Peter was present with Jesus at the raising of the synagogue ruler's daughter (Mark 5:35–41), at the Transfiguration (Mark 9:2–8), and at the arrest of Jesus in Gethsemane (Mark 14:43–50). As a representative disciple, Peter frequently typified the disciple of *little faith*. His inconsistent behavior reached a climax with his infamous denial scene (Mark 14:66–72). Peter was, however, rehabilitated in the scene where the resurrected Jesus restored Peter to his position of prominence (John 21:15–19).

Readers (vv. 2–3)

Peter addressed his readers as "God's elect" and "strangers" who were "scattered." His letter was addressed to Christian exiles who were displaced throughout much of Asia Minor. In his letter, we see Peter clearly addressing the needs of his readers. He urged them to live in accordance with the hope they had received in Christ, gave them guidance for their relationships with one another, and urged them to endure suffering joyfully for Jesus' sake. His chief aim in writing was to provide them encouragement in Christian living.

Peter

Peter's personal name means "Rock." *Simon* is often found in combination with *Peter,* reminding the reader that Simon was the earlier name and that Peter was a name given later by Jesus.

7

Tradition holds that Peter died as a martyr in Rome in the 60s. His legacy, however, lived on long after his death. To a great extent, subsequent generations of the church rely on the confession, witness, and ministry of Peter, the devoted but fallible follower of Christ.

In verses 1–2, we see each person in the Trinity at work in the salvation of God's people. God the Father *chose* through His foreknowledge. The Holy Spirit *sanctifies* believers who are *sprinkled* and thereby cleansed by the blood of Jesus.

As God set Israel apart as His own possession, He now chooses, sets apart, and cleanses those who will receive His Son.

■ *The opening verse claims Peter as author of*
■ *this letter to believers in Asia Minor. Peter's*
■ *chief aim in writing this letter is to provide*
■ *them encouragement in Christian living.*

GOD'S GREAT SALVATION (1:3–12)

CHARACTERISTICS OF GOD'S SALVATION	
Hope	v. 3
Assurance	v. 4
Faith	vv. 5, 9
Joy in spite of trials	vv. 6, 8
Praise, honor, and glory to God	v. 7
Fulfillment in lives of believers	vv. 10–12

An Inheritance (vv. 3–5)

The section 1:3–2:10 serves as a survey of the Christian life. This initial section (1:3–12) reveals the characteristics of God's salvation. God, motivated by His great mercy, has caused us to be brought from despair to a living hope.

Peter knew this living hope not as a teaching handed down from someone else. He had been snatched out of a sea of despair into which he fell when he denied Jesus three times.

Peter's firsthand experience of the Risen Christ brought him to a living hope that energized him and re-created his world.

The world of decay and death which hold most people as slaves for their entire lives no longer dominated Peter's life. For Peter and the other apostles, Jesus had demonstrated just how impotent death really is.

In witnessing the resurrection, the apostles had gotten a glimpse of the imperishable in the midst of a world that is passing away, and they were empowered to assure the generations to come of "an inheritance which is imperishable and undefiled and will not fade away, reserved in heaven for you" (v. 4).

The believers to whom Peter wrote did not have the firsthand experience of Jesus' resurrection that Peter had, but they might as well have.

Here is the secret of the resilience of Christian faith. The Holy Spirit, who raised Jesus from death, is the key Agent in the communication of the Gospel. He took the apostles' word—God's Word—and made it real in the hearts of those who heard it.

They were suffering (v. 6) and on the verge of suffering more. But they felt God's present protection and had an inward assurance of God's saving action that would appear in the future.

This assurance made them joyful—even in the midst of sufferings. Moreover, Peter reminds them that their sufferings were actually strengthening their faith and purifying it (v.7).

The Spirit's work was such that even though they had not seen Jesus in the flesh, they believed in Him and they loved him . This invisible union with their Lord caused them to "greatly rejoice with joy inexpressible and full of glory" (v. 8, NASB).

A Deliverance Foreseen by the Prophets (vv. 10–12)

Peter reminded his readers that the prophets had foretold the salvation that came in Jesus Christ. God's Spirit was at work in these prophets, causing them to search out the time and place when Messiah would come. God's Spirit showed them that Messiah must suffer and enter into glory. What they did not anticipate was the present church age that would separate the events of the Crucifixion and Resurrection from God's bringing history to a conclusion with the Second Coming of Christ.

The risen Christ, walking incognito with the Disciples on the road from Jerusalem to Emmaus, said to them: "'O foolish men and slow of heart to believe in all that the prophets have spoken! Was it not necessary for the Christ to suffer these things and to enter into His glory?' And beginning with Moses and with all the prophets, He explained to them the things concerning Himself in all the Scriptures" (Luke 24:25–27, NASB).

All aspects of God's salvation are encompassed by His grace. The salvation that God began by His grace will continue by His grace and will finally be consummated in heaven by His grace.

Through Christ, Christians can be heirs of God and "co-heirs with Christ" (Rom. 8:17; cp. Eph. 3:6). Only the book of Hebrews makes explicit use of the idea of "inheritance" as requiring the death of the testator, Christ. A "will" requires a death to come into effect, so the death of Christ keeps the new "covenant"/"will" in effect (Heb. 9:16–17).

In this passage (1 Pet. 1), the believer's inheritance is kept not on earth but in heaven. Here, "inheritance" is another name for the *salvation* "that is ready to be revealed" (v. 5).

Inheritance

In the New Testament, *inheritance* can refer to property (Luke 12:13), but most often it refers to the rewards of discipleship: (1) eternal life (e.g., Matt. 5:5; 19:29); and (2) the kingdom (e.g., Matt. 25:34).

■ *Salvation begins with the living hope estab-*
■ *lished by the resurrection of Christ from the*
■ *dead. Although believers must endure the*
■ *suffering of this present age, they have the*
■ *promise of God's protection.*

A CHALLENGE TO HOLINESS (1:13–21)

Exhortations for Holy Living (vv. 13–16)

After dealing with the fundamental matters of salvation, Peter shifted his focus to a more pastoral approach. His words in verse 13 are equivalent to saying, "Roll up your sleeves and go to work." The return of Jesus is to give Christians hope and stability in the face of persecution. They are to show their response to God's holiness by leaving the "evil desires" of their past ignorance (v. 14) and adopting God's own behavior as their pattern.

The conjunction "therefore" signals the change from statements to conclusions. Peter now exhorted his readers with several commands to guide them to a pattern of holy living.

Prepare your minds

The literal expression here is "gird up your minds." Persons living in the Mediterranean world often wore robes. When they began to move quickly, they would gather their robe up so that it wouldn't impede their progress. Peter was saying to do that to your minds.

Prepare your minds (v. 13). Believers are forbidden to lapse into intellectual slothfulness. Dullness of the mind is inexcusable and shameful. The word *mind* refers not merely to the intellect but rather to that which guides and directs one's conduct.

Be self-controlled (v. 13). The root meaning for the word *self-control* is "to be free from the influence of intoxicants." It is important to maintain a sharp mind and collected thoughts.

Set your hope (v. 13). Peter's readers are to set their hope on Christ's return. It is this hope that will give them stability and strength in midst of persecution.

Do not conform (v. 14). Each believer has a responsibility to avoid being fashioned by his or her evil desires. Instead, each must adopt God's own behavior as a pattern.

Be holy (v. 14). To be holy is to be set apart to God. Peter quoted Leviticus 11:44–45, "Be holy because I am holy." Believers, who are separated to God, are to behave in a manner that shows them to be "like" God.

God's Judgment (v. 17)

Another motivation to holiness is God's judgment. God does not judge arbitrarily or with prejudice; He judges every person's work impartially. Christians, therefore, should conduct themselves in such a way as to give evidence of God's presence.

The Price of the Cross (vv. 18–21)

Peter indicated that the proper reverence for God and an appreciation of the high cost of redemption demands holy living.

The payment that releases believers from an "empty way of life" is the "blood of Christ."

Peter noted that God had determined the performance of this work of Christ before the beginning of time. He has only recently made His plan evident in the Incarnation, Passion, and Resurrection of Jesus (v. 20).

- *Offering several commands and motivations,*
- *Peter challenged his readers to a pattern of*
- *holiness. Peter explained that the character*
- *of God and the high cost of redemption are*
- *incentives to produce holiness in his readers.*

A CALL TO HARMONY (1:22–25)

Peter again emphasized the importance of obedience. He now urged his readers to express their holiness by a deep love, from the heart, for one another. Peter's quotation from Isaiah 40:6–8 shows that the experience of this love comes from the creative activity of God.

- *Peter urged his readers to express their holi-*
- *ness by a deep love for one another. Quoting*
- *from the Old Testament, Peter showed that*
- *the experience of this love comes from the*
- *creative activity of God.*

Redemption

His readers would have understood redemption as the freeing of a slave by paying a price.

Mutual genuine love . . . love one another deeply

"Peter uses two words for 'love' in v. 22: one means brotherly love and the other divine love (*agape*). The Christian possesses brotherly love; but he needs to exert spiritual energy and love others the way God loves him. Even unsaved people can show brotherly love; it takes a Christian, controlled by the Spirit, to show *agape* love." [Taken from Warren Wiersbe, *Wiersbe's Expository Outlines on the New Testament* (Wheaton, Ill.: Victor Books, 1992), 743.]

QUESTIONS TO GUIDE YOUR STUDY

1. What is the believer's inheritance?
2. What is to be the believer's posture in the face of persecution and trial?
3. What does it mean for a Christian to be *holy*?
4. Peter provides his readers with several exhortations to be holy. What should be the believer's pattern for holy living?

The opening word of this chapter, "therefore," logically ties the reader back to the theme of being "born again" in 1:23. Because of the new birth and the new life that must follow, Peter offered his readers good advice on living the Christian life.

ADVICE FOR LIVING THE CHRISTIAN LIFE (2:1–3)

Avoiding Sin (v. 1)

Living the Christian life involves making choices, discharging responsibilities, and doing the work of the gospel. It is imperative that believers expressly avoid those things that can undermine progress in their personal and spiritual growth. Therefore, Peter charged his readers to take the responsibility of ridding from their own lives any stumbling blocks that might prevent that growth: "Rid yourselves of all malice and all deceit, hypocrisy, envy, and slander of every kind" (v. 1).

Sins That Easily Beset Us

SPECIFIC SIN	EXPANDED MEANING
All Malice	Every form of wickedness
Deceit	Not being straightforward
Hypocrisy	Forms of pretense

Sins That Easily Beset Us

SPECIFIC SIN	EXPANDED MEANING
Envy	Desiring something another possesses
All Slander	Disparaging or discrediting someone by evil speaking or backbiting

Note that not one of the sins on this list is physical. Rather, all issue from one's *mind, spirit,* and *heart.* Believers of all ages are vulnerable to each of these sins. Once this kind of sin takes hold in a believer's life, the result can be spiritually degrading and personally ruinous. Believers must absolutely and completely discard such sins. The word "rid" carries the idea of rejecting *any* connection with such sins.

"One of the most dangerous symptoms is the loss of appetite. It is the danger-signal warning that evil lurks unseen within. And there is no surer indication of religious declension and ill-health than the cessation of desire for the Word of God" [F. B. Meyer, *Tried by Fire* (London: Marshall, Morgan, and Scott, 1950), 66–67.]

Growing in the Lord (vv. 2–3)

Peter used the picture of an infant figuratively, using a word that refers to a baby that is nursing at its mother's breast. In like manner, Christians are to cultivate an appetite for nourishment—pure spiritual milk—that they may grow in their salvation.

In the New Testament, we find the word for *spiritual* "only here and in Rom. 12:1, used here with an allusion to *logou* (12:3) and *rema* (1:25), 'the sincere milk of the word' ('the milk belonging to the word,' either the milk which is the word or the milk contained in the word, that is Christ)" [A. T. Robertson, "The General Epistles," vol. 6, *Word Pictures in the New Testament*, 95].

CHRIST: THE LIVING STONE (2:4–10)

Peter used three images to describe the church in this section: living stones, a spiritual house, and a select nation.

Living Stones (vv. 4–5).

Peter portrayed the church as living stones that give sacrificial service to God. These "living stones" are believers who are built on the Living Stone, Jesus Christ. It is He who enables His followers to produce "spiritual sacrifices acceptable to God through Jesus Christ" (v. 5). Such sacrifices are those inspired by the Holy Spirit.

Our Spiritual Sacrifices to God

SACRIFICE	REFERENCE
Obedience	Rom. 12:1
Praise	Heb. 13:15–16
Practical ministry	Heb. 13:15–16

A Building (vv. 6–8)

Peter also described the church as a building or spiritual house founded on Christ as the Cornerstone. He quoted Old Testament passages from Isaiah 8:14; 28:16 and Psalm 118:22 to show that Christ is the foundation Stone for believers and a rock that causes unbelievers to trip and fall.

A Nation (vv. 9–10).

Finally, Peter used the language of Exodus 19:5–6 and Hosea 2:23 to portray believers as a select nation reflecting the glories of God (2:9–10). God had fashioned special recipients of His mercy from those who previously never belonged to anyone.

Definition of the "Church" in 1 Peter 1:9

PICTURE	EXPLANATION
"A chosen people"	Believers are the "spiritual Israel" through the new birth.
"A royal priesthood"	Because Christ is their King and Priest, believers are a royal priesthood.
"A holy nation"	The "spiritual Israel" of believers, who are God's own possession.

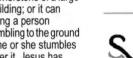

■ *Peter used three images to describe the*
■ *church: a living body, a building, and a*
■ *nation. The church built on the Living Stone,*
■ *Jesus Christ, produces spiritual sacrifices*
■ *and reflects the glories of God.*

THE PRACTICE OF GOOD WORKS (2:11–25)

Peter was eager for God's people to demonstrate distinctive, obedient behavior in order to convince critics of their faith. Over a section spanning 2:11–3:12, he urged them to apply this behavior in relation to their rulers—their earthly masters, in their families, and toward one another.

"A stone can look most unimpressive—but it can perform a vital function if made the cornerstone of a large building; or it can bring a person tumbling to the ground if he or she stumbles over it. Jesus has become the cornerstone of God's spiritual temple, and there are two possible responses. We can either take our own angle and position from the Cornerstone, and line ourselves up on him; or we can refuse to live by reference to him, and stumble over him instead. It is a vivid picture." [Stephen Motyer, *Evangelical Commentary on the Bible* (Grand Rapids: Baker Book House, 1989), 1166.]

A Call to Personal Discipline (vv. 11–12)

Peter exhorted his reader to "live . . . good lives among the pagans" (v. 12). He suggested three reasons Christians must discipline their lives:

1. Christians are foreigners to their pagan environment and not adjusted to it.
2. If Christians yield to the flesh, they will wage battle against their best selves.
3. Self-discipline and obedience have a wholesome influence on unbelievers.

Submission to Government Authorities (vv. 13–17)

Believers are to practice responsible citizenship by submitting to "every authority instituted among men" (v. 13). Peter urged voluntary submission on the part of believers for the purpose of commending Jesus' lordship. At this point he picked up on the theme of freedom. Christians are responsibly free to "love the brotherhood of believers, fear God, honor the king" (that is, their political leaders).

Submission of Servants to Masters (vv. 18–25)

Peter's era was one in which slavery was an accepted part of the social system. From the earliest times, the Roman government accepted and promoted the practice. In the Roman world, treatment of slaves varied considerably. By the first century, however, the institution of slavery was changing. Public sentiment decried harsh treatment of slaves, and many leading orators spoke against the institution. Christianity arose in a real-life, tension-filled setting. The slaves' insurrections had already failed, causing significant injury, sorrow, and loss of life. Working within these tensions, however, the seeds of abolition were sown.

"In today's world where slavery has been almost universally abolished and where the actual terms 'servants' and 'master' have been dropped from most vocabularies, what does this passage mean? Christians, no matter whom we are accountable to, are obligated to do our work responsibly. We are obligated to maintain the kind of relationship to those to whom we are accountable and to those who may be accountable to us that will conform to the example set by Christ. Paul states this same point, 'Whatever your task, work heartily, as serving the Lord (Col. 3:23).'" [Foy Valentine, *1 & 2 Peter*, vol. 23 of *Layman's Bible Book Commentary*, 105.]

As servants responded to the gospel of Jesus Christ, it became imperative for church leaders to address the issues of servant-master relationships. In the New Testament, we find both Peter and the apostle Paul providing guidance on this subject.

Peter provided special counsel to those who are servants of slave owners. Slaves are to be subject to their masters and submit to them with all respect. The incentive for showing this kind of subjection, even in the presence of provocation, is the moving example of Christ's obedience. As Christ suffered for all, also as His followers, Christians may be called to suffer wrongfully for doing right.

CHRIST AS THE EXAMPLE OF RIGHTEOUSNESS (2:21–25)

Although directed primarily to slaves, Peter's counsel about submission to masters in this section has rich contemporary application.

Righteous living in daily existence is made possible because of Christ's sacrifice. He is now the believer's Shepherd who cares for His sheep in every area and relationship of life (v. 25). Jesus is the believer's example of righteousness lived out in daily life. Through His power believers may follow "in his steps" (v. 21).

■ *Peter was eager for God's people to demon-*
■ *strate distinctive, obedient behavior in order*
■ *to convince critics of their faith. He urged*
■ *them to apply this behavior in relation to*
■ *their rulers and their earthly masters.*

QUESTIONS TO GUIDE YOUR STUDY

1. Peter presented a list of certain sins that can easily beset us. What is unique about these sins?

2. Peter described three images that picture the church. What do we learn from these?

3. What is the believer's incentive for submitting to authority?

4. In verse 25, Peter stated that Jesus is the Shepherd and Overseer of our souls. What are the implications of his statement? What other biblical truths can you think of that support that statement?

Peter continued his theme of submission from chapter 2 and emphasized the need for submission in three areas of the believer's life: in the home, in the midst of suffering, and toward Christ.

SUBMISSION IN THE HOME (3:1–7)

This section is one of the most intensely practical parts of Peter's letter. It is helpful to read and compare what other portions of the New Testament has to say on the subject. The apostle Paul had a good deal to say about the subject of marital relationships in his writings. (See the chart for these parallel passages.)

PAUL'S WRITINGS
ON THE MARITAL RELATIONSHIP

Eph. 5:22–6:4

Col. 3:18–21

1 Cor. 7:1–17

1 Tim. 2:8–15

Although it in no way diminishes the authority of God's Word, often it has been pointed out that Paul himself was not married. Peter, however, was married. In his Gospel, Matthew referred to Peter's wife's mother, who had a fever and was healed by Jesus (8:14–15).

Counsel to Wives (vv. 1–6)

As Peter counseled servants to be submissive to their masters, so he counseled wives "to be submissive" to their husbands. The term *submit* means "to subject or subordinate." A matter to

"Submission is voluntarily cooperating with someone, first out of love and respect for God and then out of love and respect for that person. Submitting to nonbelievers is difficult, but it is a vital part of leading them to Jesus Christ. We are not called to submit to nonbelievers to the point that we compromise our relationship with God, but we must look for every opportunity to humbly serve in the power of God's Spirit." [*Life Application Study Bible* (Wheaton: Tyndale House Publishers, Inc., 1996), p. 2001.]

note is that in the biblical passages dealing with the submission of the wife, the nature of the wife's submission is different from the submission of children or slaves. Children and slaves are told to obey; the wife is not. The wife has a different relationship to her husband than children to parents or slaves to masters. The motivation for voluntary submission is that it is a proper Christian attitude.

In these verses, Peter had in mind here a situation where the husband is not a believer. Wives are to be submissive so that if her husband does "not believe the word," he may be "won over without words by the behavior" of his wife.

The submission Peter counseled wives to observe in relationship to their husbands reflects the acceptance of the husband-wife relationship, which, like the acceptance of human slavery, prevailed throughout the world of Peter's day. The power of the Christian gospel was just beginning to work on behalf of slaves, government, and women. At the time of Peter's writing of his letter to Asia Minor, there had been insufficient time for the Gospel to change significantly the established and structured institutions of society.

Counsel to Husbands (v. 7)

The apostle also had a word for husbands. Christian husbands are to recognize their wives as "heirs" of the gracious gift of life. Peter was affirming here that marriage is indeed a partnership. Husbands are to live in understanding of their wives, maintaining a considerate spirit, kindness, and honor to them. To fail in this area will result in an ineffective prayer life.

The weaker partner

The phrase "weaker partner" is a reference to the physical body. According to A. T. Robertson, "She is termed 'the weaker,' not for intellectual or moral weakness, but purely for physical reasons, which the husband must recognize with due consideration for marital happiness." ["The General Epistles," vol. 6, *Word Pictures in the New Testament*, 111.]

■ *Peter continues his theme of submission,*
■ *focusing on submission within the marital*
■ *relationship. Marriage is a partnership that*
■ *demands submission from the wife and lov-*
■ *ing understanding and consideration from*
■ *the husband.*

SUBMISSION IN THE MIDST OF SUFFERING (3:8–17)

Living in Harmony with One Another (vv. 8–13)

Here Peter discussed the mutual love between his readers and the harmony that should prevail: "live in harmony with one another" (v. 8). He urged them to practice vital qualities of the Christian life that will lead to this harmony.

Peter summed up this section by quoting Psalm 34:12–16, one of the great passages of Scripture that encourages us to be "eager to do good" (v. 13).

Suffering Persecution (v. 14)

Believers who are faithful to Christ and His teachings may expect suffering. It should not come as a surprise to those who follow Christ, who is our example in suffering. When suffering does come, Peter said, "If you suffer for what is right, you are blessed" (v. 14). Eventually, those who persecute will "be ashamed of their slander" (v. 16).

The New Testament speaks clearly about the certainty of believers suffering persecution for their faith. Several writers deal with the subject. The following chart highlights a few of those passages.

The Church in Harmony

COMMAND	EXPANDED MEANING
"Live in harmony" (v. 8).	Having a unity of spirit and attitude in spiritual matters.
"Be sympathetic" (v. 8).	Sharing in the feelings of others, whether in sorrow or in joy.
"Love as brothers" (v. 8).	Expressing brotherly and sisterly love among God's people.
"Be compassionate and humble" (v. 8).	Being tenderhearted or good-hearted toward others with a humble spirit.
"Do not repay evil with evil" (v. 9).	Repaying acts of evil with acts of blessing.

We are to prepare ourselves for trials and tribulations that come from a hostile world, not simply by hardening our minds or steeling our wills but by immersing ourselves in righteousness. It is that unqualified and uncompromised righteousness before God and others that is the Christian's finest armor against the attack of persecution.

Dealing with Persecution (vv. 15–17)

Believers are not to fear those who persecute them. Rather, they are to "set apart Christ as Lord." In verse 15, Peter provided two steps a believer may take to respond righteously to those who persecute them:

1. Be prepared to give an answer.
2. Maintain a spirit of gentleness and respect.

By practicing these steps, the Christian will keep a clear conscience because of his or her behavior, and the accuser or accusers will be put to shame for their slander.

The Persecution of the Saints

REFERENCE	SPEAKER OR WRITER	KEY TRUTH
Jas. 4:4	James	"Don't you know that friendship with the world is hatred toward God?"
2 Tim. 3:12	Paul	"Everyone who wants to live a godly life in Christ Jesus will be persecuted."
John 16:33	Jesus	"In this world you will have trouble. But take heart! I have overcome the world."

- Believers who are faithful to Christ and His
- teachings may expect suffering. They may
- prepare themselves for times of suffering by
- immersing themselves in the righteousness of
- Christ.

SUBMISSION TO CHRIST (3:18–22)

Jesus: The Believer's Example in Suffering (v. 18)

Christ is the believer's best example of how to bear suffering for the sake of righteousness. His

"There is a sense, of course, in which our Saviour suffered for our sins *once* . . . . But we must not suppose that Jesus has passed into an unsuffering heaven. He still suffers in each of his members. He is crucified afresh when we yield to willful sins. He travails in birth until his kingdom come. He is touched with the feeling of our infirmities. How can He be at rest, whilst his beloved are tossing in the storm, and the members of his bride are not complete? And through his sufferings blessing is accruing; they cannot be in vain: we shall all see soon; meanwhile let us bear fellowship with Him in his anguish, drinking of his cup, that we may share his glory." [F. B. Meyer, *Tried by Fire*, 123–24.]

example should encourage us to endure our own suffering patiently.

"The Spirits in Prison" (vv. 19–20)

Some have interpreted the spirits in prison to mean departed human spirits. But the word for spirits, *pneumata,* is never used in the Bible to refer to human spirits. More likely is that these are the spirits of fallen angels to whom Jesus announced His victory over evil and their own judgment.

Christian Baptism (vv. 21–22)

Peter ties the account of Noah's Ark to Christian baptism. The Flood is a picture of judgment. The ark is salvation, deliverance of Noah and his family from God's judgment. Baptism is a picture which tells forth the death, burial, and Resurrection of Christ. These events, pictured by baptism, are the ark through which believers are saved from the judgment of God which fell on Christ.

Preached

The word Peter uses for "preaching" (*kerusso*) to the spirits in prison is not the same word the New Testament used for "preaching the gospel" (*euangelizo*). Peter opted for a word that means "to proclaim" or "to announce." Jesus' act of "preaching" following His resurrection was a proclamation of His *victory* to the fallen angels in Hades rather than a proclamation of the gospel.

■ *As believers we show our submission to*
■ *Christ by following His example in our suf-*
■ *fering as well as in the act of Christian bap-*
■ *tism. Even the fallen angels in Hades must*
■ *recognize and submit to the authority of the*
■ *resurrected Christ.*

QUESTIONS TO GUIDE YOUR STUDY

1. Peter spoke of marital relationships. What is the responsibility of the wife? of the husband? What do other New Testament writers have to say about the subject?

2. What should be the view of Christians with regard to suffering? What steps can believers take to remain submissive to

Christ during times of persecution and suffering?

3. One of most difficult passages for interpreters over the years has been 1 Peter 1:19–20. What do you think Peter meant by his statement that Jesus "preached to the spirits in prison"?

4. Why did Peter tie in Christian baptism with Noah and the Flood? What was he teaching here?

This chapter opens with the word *therefore,* which introduces the reader to the main lesson to be drawn from the previous section, 3:18–22. Both this chapter and chapter 5 treat the general theme of God's grace in the midst suffering. Indeed, in 4:12 Peter spoke of a "painful trial" ("fiery ordeal," NRSV), persecution that some were already suffering and which others would soon suffer.

LIVING IN THE WILL OF GOD (4:1–6)

Suffering with Christ (v. 1)

One of the Christian's great challenges is to "arm" oneself with the same attitude as that of Christ toward suffering. Jesus said, "Whoever finds his life will lose it, and whoever loses his life for my sake will find it" (Matt. 10:39). In the Gospels, we have a representative record of how Jesus dealt with life's challenges and responsibilities. His attitudes and approaches are the believer's ideal.

Redeeming the Time (vv. 2–3)

As believers live for the will of God, their values change; and they align their lives with God's desires, the stated principles and commands in His Word. For the Christian, life's deepest concern is not what human appetites desire but what God's will dictates. Life becomes a precious resource that cannot be wasted by "doing what the pagans choose to do" (v. 3).

Relating to God's Judgment (vv. 4–6)

Because Christians do not join in practicing sin with the world, the world abuses them. Believers may take comfort in knowing that God will someday judge such people.

Arm

The word *arm* means "to equip" or "to arm" oneself. It is part of the New Testament motif of the Christian soldier (see Eph. 6:10–18). Although this word is used only here in the New Testament, it was used in classical Greek, where its usage provides insight into what Peter had in mind and his readers understood.

For example, to arm oneself was to prepare by acquiring the necessary provisions for the way, such as a meal, lamps, horses, and ships. One usage even speaks of one arming himself with the attribute of *boldness*. Here, Peter was urging believers to arm themselves with the same attitude Christ had toward suffering. That includes aligning with His stated thoughts and convictions about the topic. [See G. Kittel and G. Friedrich, *Theological Dictionary of the New Testament* (Grand Rapids: Eerdmans, 1967), 5:294–95.]

Some have misinterpreted the words of verse 6, "The gospel was preached even to those who are now dead," to suggest that unbelievers who die will have an opportunity to hear and respond to the gospel message after death. There is no hint in the Bible of a second chance after death. Rather, Peter was speaking of believers who had died and were enjoying spiritual life with God in heaven. Warren Wiersbe offered a paraphrase that provides insight for this complex passage:

Verse 6 may be paraphrased this way: "There are people now dead physically, but alive with God in the spirit, who were judged by the world. But they heard the Gospel before they died and believed. They suffered and died because of their faith—but they are living with God! It is better to suffer for Christ and to be with God than to follow the world and be lost." [Warren W. Wiersbe, *Wiersbe's Expository Outlines on the New Testament* (Wheaton, Ill.: Victor Books, 1992), p. 751.]

■ *Peter urged a full commitment by believers to*
■ *the will of God. Arming themselves with the*
■ *same attitude that Christ had toward suffer-*
■ *ing is a starting point. They are then to live*
■ *out the rest of life controlled not by their*
■ *"evil human desires," but by the will of God.*

LIVING THAT GLORIFIES GOD (4:7–11)

"The end of all things is near" is a reference to the end of history, or this present age. This emphasis on the expected end of the age is shared by the apostle Paul in his writings. It is also found in the books of Matthew, Hebrews, James, Mark, and Revelation.

Early Christians and the New Testament writers viewed the early return of Christ as a challenge to maintain a moral lifestyle. This ought to be the case for believers today. In view of the expected return of Christ ("therefore"), Peter set forth several exhortations that serve as guidelines for living a life that brings glory to God.

"Be clear-minded and self-controlled." A clear mind and self-control are essential to effective, focused praying. An active and effective prayer life should characterize all believers anticipating Jesus' return.

"Love each other deeply." The love Peter spoke about here is a strenuous, intense love. It is an unselfish love that stretches to reach to the other without breaking.

Use your gift. The nearness of the Lord's coming should lead believers to make vigorous use of their spiritual gifts.

Living That Glorifies God

Exhortation	Reason
"Be clear-minded and self-controlled."	For effective prayer
"Love each other deeply."	Love restores and reconciles
"Offer hospitality."	To serve others
"Use your gift."	To glorify God

"Offer hospitality."

Hospitality was a ministry during the time of the early church. But this practice was by no means limited to the church. And Eastern hospitality was not merely a custom; it was a sacred duty that everyone was expected to observe. Believers would entertain or receive strangers as well as traveling missionaries. In doing so, they would provide their guests with food, shelter, and protection. Christians ought to be ready always to extend hospitality and minister to the needs of others.

■ *Early Christians viewed the return of Christ*
■ *as a challenge to maintain a moral lifestyle.*
■ *This ought also to be the case for believers*
■ *today. In view of the expected return of*
■ *Christ, Peter set forth several exhortations*
■ *that serve as guidelines for living a life that*
■ *brings glory to God.*

LIVING UNDER SUFFERING (4:12–19)

Peter presented a threefold perspective to encourage his readers not to be surprised at the prospect of the painful trial that lay ahead.

Painful trial

This word (one word in the Greek text) translated "painful trial" (NIV) is more graphically translated "fiery ordeal" in the NRSV. This word is often used in a purifying or refining sense, which is the case here as Peter referred to the "fiery ordeal" as a "test" (NRSV). Used metaphorically, such an ordeal is truly a "trial by fire."

Sharing in Christ's Suffering (vv. 12–13)

The NRSV renders an excellent translation of verse 12: "Beloved, do not be surprised at the fiery ordeal that is taking place among you to test you, as though something strange were happening to you."

Peter reminded his readers that their suffering could lead them to share in Christ's own experiences, a development that would link them more closely with their Savior. The "fiery ordeal" is a test, which by purifying and refining them, will make them more like Jesus.

Suffering and Special Blessing (vv. 14–16)

Peter suggests to his readers that their bearing insults for the name of Christ could lead to a richer supply of the Holy Spirit in their lives: "If you are insulted because of the name of Christ, you are blessed, for the Spirit of glory and of God rests on you" (v. 14). The "glow" of God's glory on the believer will certainly be a witness to those who persecute God's people.

Suffering as a Witness to Unbelievers (vv. 17–18)

"For it is time for judgment to begin with the family of God" (v. 17). Although the time had come for persecution to fall on the church, the final outcome for God's people will be victory. The final judgment of unbelievers, however, is left fearfully hanging: "What will be the outcome for those who do not obey the gospel of God?" In other words, what will happen when the time comes for unbelievers to be judged?

Suffering and God's Faithfulness (v. 19)

Peter closed this chapter by providing his readers the motivation for their obedient, trusting service. Peter reminded them that God is their faithful Creator. Based on His proven faithfulness, when Christians "suffer according to God's will," they are to commit themselves to Him and continue to do good.

Commit themselves

The phrase "commit themselves" is a compound word made up of the preposition "over" and the verb "to place or lay." The word is a banking figure meaning "to deposit" (as in 1 Tim. 1:18; 2 Tim. 2:2). In the context of this passage, 1 Peter 4:19, it means "to give over oneself," "to entrust oneself," or "to commit to one's charge." It is the very word Jesus used as He died on the cross (Luke 23:46): "Father, into your hands I commit my spirit." ["The General Epistles," vol. 6, *Word Pictures in the New Testament*, 129.]

■ *Peter presented a threefold perspective to*
■ *encourage his readers not to be surprised at the*
■ *prospect of the painful trial that lay ahead: (1)*
■ *they would share in Christ's sufferings; (2)*
■ *they could have a richer supply of the Holy*
■ *Spirit in their lives; and (3) their motivation for*
■ *obedience is the faithfulness of God.*

QUESTIONS TO GUIDE YOUR STUDY

1. What does it mean for Christians to "arm themselves" with Christ's attitude toward suffering? How does one do this?

2. What guidelines did Peter set forth for living a life that brings glory to God?

3. Why does God allow "fiery ordeals" in our lives? What good comes from them?

4. When Christians suffer according to God's will, what does it mean to "commit" oneself to God?

In this final chapter, Peter focused on directives to church leaders and general exhortations and warnings to all Christians. After a short preaching section, he closed his letter with a final greeting.

ASSURANCES FOR FAITHFUL SERVANTS (5:1–11)

To Elders (vv. 1–4)

This first exhortation is to elders in the churches. Peter himself was a fellow elder. The purpose of this part of the letter, however, was not to discuss the duties of elders. Rather, he was addressing the elders as *older* church leaders and urged them to be faithful shepherds from a willing heart with a desire to serve as an example to the flock.

To Younger Christians (v. 5)

As elders have responsibilities, so do younger members of the church. Peter charged them to "be submissive" to the elders. The submission Peter spoke of here is most likely a reference to the recognition that the younger people have much to learn from the older believers in the church. Inexperienced young people in the church should profit from older members' experiences. In addition, exuberance and enthusiasm can be properly directed and channeled by older believer's experience and wisdom.

Peter especially exhorted younger believers to "clothe" themselves with humility toward one another. He then quoted Proverbs 3:34: "God opposes the proud but gives grace to the humble."

Cast all your anxiety on him

The word translated "cast upon" is a compound word in Greek. It is a construction of the preposition "upon" and the verb "to hurl, to throw off." The basic meaning of this word in 1 Peter 5:7 is "to throw onto." "Subjection to God's lordship is demonstrated in the fact that the community casts all its care on the Lord and is thus relieved of its burden." [G. Kittel and G. Friedrich, *Theological Dictionary of the New Testament* (Grand Rapids: Eerdmans, 1968), 6:994.]

To the Faithful Who Persevere (vv. 6–11)

Now directing his words to all believers, Peter encouraged them to persevere by cultivating the following special qualities of the Christian life.

"Humble yourselves" (v. 6). Peter urged his readers to practice humility. Those who humble themselves under "God's mighty hand" may do so with the assurance that God will "lift them up" when the time is just right.

"Cast all your anxiety on him" (v. 7). Rather than wait for God to take the initiative and remove those anxieties troubling their hearts, believers are to take the responsibility of casting their anxieties upon him.

"Be self-controlled and alert" (v. 8). These two imperatives are strong exhortations to not be slack in remaining watchful. Although we may be confident in God's care for us, we must ever be vigilant. Christians are in the midst of constant spiritual warfare and are the targets of Satan's attacks. Peter depicted the enemy as prowling around "like a roaring lion looking for someone to devour" (v. 8).

"Resist him, standing firm in the faith" (v. 9). Christians who are tempted or threatened by the devil's evil presence are to "resist" him. Believers may stand against the devil and firm in the faith, taking comfort that other believers throughout the world are experiencing the same kind of suffering.

■ *Peter encouraged persevering believers to*
■ *cultivate special qualities of the Christian*
■ *life. They are to exercise humility, give their*
■ *anxieties to God, and to be alert for the*
■ *attacks of the enemy. It is important that*
■ *believers not be slack in their vigilance and*
■ *that they stand against the wiles of the devil.*

CONCLUSION (5:12–14)

Final Greetings (vv. 12–14a)

Peter's summary of his purpose is: "I have written to you briefly, encouraging you and testifying that this is the true grace of God" (v. 12). Even in his closing words, he continued to admonish his readers to "stand fast" in their Christian lives. He then sent greetings from those at his location, referring to it as "Babylon."

Benediction (v. 14b)

With a simple but powerful statement, Peter concluded his letter: "Peace to all of you who are in Christ." It is a statement of unity which underscores the message of his letter.

Babylon

It is generally believed that the "Babylon" mentioned here is Rome. 'The use of the code name for Rome was widespread among early Christians, particularly after the waves of persecution began to emanate from the city of the Caesars'" [Foy Valentine, *1, 2 Peter*, vol. 23 of *Layman's Bible Book Commentary*, 119–20.]

■ *Peter concluded his letter by exhorting his*
■ *readers to stand fast in their Christian lives.*
■ *This is especially significant as waves of per-*
■ *secution from Rome against the church had*
■ *already begun.*

QUESTIONS TO GUIDE YOUR STUDY

  1. What exhortations did Peter give to the elders of the churches. To the younger believers?

2. What special qualities of the Christian life did Peter encourage the persevering faithful to cultivate?

3. What does it mean for Christians to cast their anxiety onto God? What does it involve?

4. What can a Christian do to prepare against the attacks of the devil?

INTRODUCTION
2 PETER

Peter wrote his second letter to counter the influence of heresy within the church (2 Pet. 2:1). He appealed for spiritual growth as an antidote to defeat the heretics who had infiltrated the community and urged his readers to live holy lives in anticipation of Jesus' return (2 Pet. 3:11–12). It is a message of pastoral encouragement, support for living the Christian life, prophetic warning against false doctrine, and concern for the proper preparation for a day of judgment.

Second Peter is brief, more like a short sermon or an essay than an actual letter. The brevity of this letter resulted in its being ignored for centuries by the church. Few Christians made use of it until the time of Origen (A.D. 250).

2 Peter in a "Nutshell"

PURPOSE:	ENCOURAGEMENT FOR PERSECUTED AND SUFFERING CHRISTIANS
Major Doctrine:	Knowledge; the influence of Scripture
Key Passage:	2 Peter 1:16–21
Other Key Doctrines:	Judgment; practical Christian living; spiritual growth

AUTHOR

The author claimed to be Peter in 1:1 and asserted that he was an eyewitness to the Transfiguration (1:16–18). His claim to be an apostle and his admission of friendship to Paul (3:15) clearly indicates that the writer intended to be seen as Peter.

PURPOSE FOR WRITING

Peter felt strongly that his death was near (2 Pet. 1:14–15). He wanted to leave a spiritual testament to provide helpful instruction after his departure. He warned against the character and false teachings of heretics who would infiltrate the church (2:1–19; 3:1–4). To provide protection against errors, he urged a development of Christian virtues (1:3–11) and constant growth in God's grace (3:17–18).

DATE AND PLACE OF WRITING

Date. Peter anticipated that his death would be soon (1:14–15). Assuming Peter wrote both 1 and 2 Peter, we can observe that Peter called this his second writing to the same readers (3:1). There is little specific information by which to arrive at an exact date, but it seems likely that 2 Peter was written shortly after 1 Peter. A time in the mid-to-late 60s, shortly before Peter's death seems likely.

Place. Peter's letter contains little indication of his location. We may leave this as an open question, for a decision on this issue does not affect one's interpretation of the letter.

AUDIENCE

The letter lacks a specific address, something that 1 Peter does contain. So other data must be considered. If we assume that Peter wrote the letter, "my second letter" (3:1) would indicate that he was writing to the same group who had received the first letter. The statement of 1:16 suggests that Peter had spoken or preached to this group, but we have no knowledge of when or how this occurred. It seems best to suggest that Peter wrote to churches located in the northern part of Asia Minor.

Eusebius places Peter's death in the fourteenth year of Nero that is variously dated from A.D. 64 to 68.

LITERARY FORM

Several passages in 2 Peter indicate that Peter wrote to a specific congregation (1:16; 2:1; 3:1). The entire letter is an earnest warning against false teachers and an appeal for growth in maturity. Peter made little use of the Old Testament in quotations (but see 2:22), yet there are frequent allusions to Old Testament characters and events (2:4–8).

THE THEOLOGY OF 2 PETER

Peter held to a high view of Scripture (1:19–21), and he viewed Paul's writings as "Scripture" (3:16). He designated Jesus Christ as "Savior" and "Lord" (1:1–2), and he outlined his observation of Jesus' Transfiguration (1:6–8). He affirmed the return of Christ (3:1–4) and asserted God's sovereign control of the events of history (3:13). He used the certainty of Christ's return as an incentive to appeal for godly living (3:14).

BASIC OUTLINE FOR 2 PETER

  I. Greetings (1:1–2)
 II. Provisions for Spiritual Growth (1:3–21)
III. The Danger of False Teaching (2:1–22)
IV. A Reminder of God's Hope (3:1–3)
 V. Closing Commands (3:14–18)

QUESTIONS TO GUIDE YOUR STUDY

1. What was Peter's purpose for writing this letter?
2. Who was his audience? We don't know where Peter was when he wrote this letter. Is this a problem for our understanding its message?
3. What is Peter's main theme of this letter?
4. In his letter, Peter sought to protect his readers from the errors of false teachers. From what can be seen in the introductory material here, what tact did Peter follow to prepare his readers?

2 PETER 1 ················

The theme of this chapter is Christ's return. Peter gave final warning against the false teachers and provided his readers assurance and encouragement. In the last chapter of this letter, he closed with advice to the faithful in view of the coming judgment.

SALUTATION (1:1–2)

Peter identified himself as a servant and an apostle of Jesus Christ. His salutation here and the one in 1 Peter differ in two ways: (1) here Peter used his full name, Simon Peter; and (2) although he did not address his letter to a specific geographic location, his references in 1:16; 2:1; and 3:1 suggest that he had a specific congregation in mind.

Peter addressed his letter to those who had "received faith" in Christ. This faith is a precious gift shared by Peter and those to whom he wrote. Such faith is imparted by "the righteousness of our God and Savior, Jesus Christ."

It is evident that Peter wanted his readers to experience God's loving favor and spiritual wholeness because of their clear, personal knowledge of Jesus.

PROVISIONS FOR SPIRITUAL GROWTH (1:3–4)

Peter reminded his readers that God not only provides faith but also provides everything they need for spiritual life and godly living. These gifts come through knowledge of God.

In this chapter he provided four sources of power, or incentives, for spiritual development in his readers: (1) God's calling and election;

Righteousness

Righteousness is an attribute of God. God is righteous. God also works to make things right, and in this latter sense, God's rightousness imparts the gift of faith to sinful human beings.

Peter may have been writing to combat a gnosticlike teaching that said that, in addition to knowledge of Christ, believers needed to learn a hidden knowledge which contains the key to spiritual growth.

Given

The word translated "given" uses a tense in the Greek New Testament that emphasizes the continuing nature of what is given. Therefore, the spiritual resources God gives to believers are continually available to them as reliable sources of strength and growth.

(2) Peter's witness to his readers; (3) God's majestic glory; and (4) the prophetic message of Scripture.

God's intended result of these provisions is that "through these he has given us his very great and precious promises, so that through them you may participate in the divine nature and escape the corruption in the world caused by evil desires" (v. 4).

■ *Living the Christian life does not depend on*
■ *one's own strength and resources. Here Peter*
■ *reminded his readers that God provides*
■ *everything believers need for spiritual life*
■ *and godly living.*

A CALL TO MORAL AND SPIRITUAL DEVELOPMENT (1:5–11)

Many refer to this section as the "ladder of faith." It teaches a progressive growth from the foundation of faith to the greatest of the ethical qualities for which Christians are to strive—love. Peter taught that believers need to strive to "supplement" or add to their saving faith. The most debilitating sin of modern believers is the failure to go on to maturity in Christ.

In verses 6–7, Peter showed that each quality builds on the previous one. Believers are never to pause in their upward climb until they have supplemented:

Add

The word translated "add" is a compound word in the Greek New Testament. It is made up of the preposition "upon" attached to the verb "to place." The preposition in compound words like this often makes the verb to which it is attached emphatic, thereby creating a new word with a unique meaning. Here the word seems to have taken on an accumulative force, which carries the idea of increasing and adding to the supplies. This word is often translated "put upon," "supplement," or "add."

- faith with virtue
- virtue with knowledge
- knowledge with self-control
- self-control with steadfastness
- steadfastness with godliness

- godliness with brotherly affection
- brotherly affection with love

Love is faith's finished product. "God is love" (1 John 4:16); therefore, Christians are to "be like him" (1 John 3:2).

The Ladder of Moral Development

RUNG OF THE LADDER	EXTENDED MEANING
Love	Self-giving for the good of others
Brotherly affection	Love for brothers and sisters in Christ
Godliness	Quality of being like God in daily life
Steadfastness	Endurance, perseverance, and courageous patience
Self-control	Mastery of self and control of one's appetites and drives
Knowledge	Practical understanding of the truth
Virtue	Moral excellence
Faith	Saving faith in God

- *Peter taught a progressive growth from the*
- *foundation of faith to the greatest of the eth-*
- *ical qualities for which Christians are to*
- *strive—love. Peter taught that believers need*
- *to strive to supplement or add these qualities*
- *to their saving faith.*

COUNSEL FOR CONTINUED SPIRITUAL GROWTH (1:12–21)

The Transfiguration

The Transfiguration was an open display for the disciples of the glory Jesus had before the Incarnation. It was also a foreshadowing of His Resurrection and return. This event occurred most likely on Mount Hermon (elevation, 9,100 ft.). It is full of meaning, as much that took place there was highly symbolic. A mountain was often a place of revelation. Also present at the Transfiguration were Moses and Elijah. They represented the Law and the Prophets respectively, which testify to but must give way to Jesus. The Transfiguration experience provided needed reassurance for the disciples as they contemplated Jesus' death and their own future suffering.

More Incentives to Spiritual Growth (vv. 12–19)

Peter began this section by refreshing the memory of his readers. Although they are "firmly established in the truth," Peter saw value in bringing to remembrance those things that would cause them to develop the qualities he had just mentioned and to grow spiritually. At this point, Peter was convinced that his death was approaching (he spoke of his "departure"). From his remarks in verse 15, it appears that he intended for his letter to continue to be circulated generally.

Peter now elaborated on two more incentives for the spiritual growth of his readers: God's glory and the prophetic message of Scripture.

God's Glory. The recipients of 2 Peter likely encountered those who mocked the idea of a powerful, heavenly Christ who could strengthen them for godly living. Peter had been an eyewitness of Christ's majesty in the Transfiguration. He could testify that the glory of Jesus was a reality they could experience.

The Prophetic Message of Scripture. The final incentive Peter provided in this passage is the

Incentives for Spiritual Growth in Chapter 1

PROVISION	PASSAGE
1. God's calling and election	1:3–11
2. Peter's witness	1:12–15
3. The glory of God	1:16–18
4. The prophetic message of Scripture	1:19–21

prophetic message of Scripture. Peter felt that the Transfiguration and other events in Jesus' life made the scriptural picture of Jesus more sure and certain. Christians are able to find guidance from this word until Christ returns in person. Peter stated that Scripture is reliable because it has a divine rather than a human origin.

Paul wrote to Timothy: "All Scripture is inspired by God and is useful to teach us what is true and to make us realize what is wrong in our lives. It straightens us out and teaches us to do what is right."

2 Timothy 3:16, NLT

The "Prophecy of Scripture" (vv. 20–21)

This passage has been understood variously. Among the views that have been advanced are:

1. Scripture should not be interpreted according to one's own bias.
2. Scripture cannot be interpreted properly without the Holy Spirit.
3. Scripture cannot be interpreted apart from the rest of Scripture.
4. The prophecies did not originate from the prophets but from God.

While all those views may have a measure of validity, the grammar of the underlying Greek text of our English translation seems to favor the last view. It suggests that Peter was speaking more about the source of Scripture than its proper interpretation. As believers, we can be certain that the Scriptures are of divine origin, not human.

- *Convinced that his death was approaching,*
- *Peter reminded his readers about the quali-*
- *ties they should be developing in the course*
- *of their spiritual growth. Bringing to remem-*
- *brance God's glory and the prophetic mes-*
- *sage of Scripture are powerful incentives.*

QUESTIONS TO GUIDE YOUR STUDY

1. Describe the "ladder of faith" that Peter provided in this chapter. Where does it start? Where does it lead?
2. What did Peter mean by "adding" or "supplementing" to one's faith?
3. Peter mentioned his Transfiguration experience with Jesus. Why did this event mean so much to Peter?
4. What was Peter saying to his readers in 1:20–21?

Christianity has always been plagued by false teachers and false teachings. During the occasion of this letter, Peter's readers currently were under threat by false teachers "among" them. In this chapter Peter instructed his readers about the infiltrators and issued warnings against deceivers and false teachers.

THE AGENDA OF FALSE TEACHERS (2:1–3)

They Deny Christ (v. 1)

False teachers introduce "destructive heresies." These heresies are clever arguments against the true deity of Jesus Christ or persuasive contention against the true humanity of Christ. Both kinds of heresies sprang up among the early Christians. Heresies have reared their ugly heads many times over the centuries, and even today their modern counterparts are alive and active among Christians.

They Falsely Lead Others (v. 2)

The denial of Christ leads to immorality. False teachers are characterized by immorality and greed. Both of those sins have a common source in the rejection of God's will. "Many will follow their shameful ways."

As a result of the influence of false teachers, many people are enticed into blatant immoralities. In opposition to the teachings and activities of those heretics, the Bible teaches that Jesus is "the way, the truth, and the life" (John 14:6). A denial of Jesus leads to a denial of His way of truth and His moral uprightness.

Heresy

A *heresy* is an opinion or doctrine not in line with the accepted teaching of a church, the opposite of orthodoxy. It is clear that in the New Testament, the concept of heresy had more to do with fellowship within the church than with doctrinal teachings. While New Testament writers were certainly concerned about false teachings, they apparently were just as disturbed by improper attitudes.

In the writings of Ignatius, a leader of the church in the early second century, the word *heresy* takes on a technical meaning. Most frequently in the writings of the early church fathers, the heresy about which they were most concerned was Gnosticism, a teaching that denied that Jesus was fully human.

Those leaders who deny Christ and practice sexual corruption and depravity bring "the way of truth into disrepute" (v. 2). Those believers who follow false leaders and their teachings shamefully compromise their Christian witness and become ineffective witnesses for Christ.

They Exploit the Weak (v. 3)

False teachers are deceivers and seducers, not disciples. They invent stories, which they use to exploit the weak. Their motivation is greed. When their deception works, they lure unwary believers away from Christ and into lust. Words have enormous power; they can be used to bless or curse. It is paramount that Christians speak God's truth in love and avoid using false words or "inventing stories."

- *Peter explained the agenda of false teachers.*
- *Their activity is destructive. They deny Christ,*
- *falsely lead others, and exploit the weak.*

THE DESTINY OF THOSE WHO DENY CHRIST (2:4–10a)

In this section Peter used Old Testament examples of judgment on sin to show the certainty of punishment for followers of false teachers. This group of verses (4–10a) is a long, complete sentence that needs to be studied as a unit. Peter illustrated the destiny of the disobedient with illustrations from three historical events: (1) the casting out of fallen angels; (2) the Flood; and (3) Sodom and Gomorrah.

The Fallen Angels (v. 4)

This illustration involves God's condemnation of the fallen angels who sinned and were cast out of heaven. Some believe this event refers to "the sons of God" in Genesis 6:2. Revelation 12:7–12 indicates that rebellious angels long ago were cast out of their specials places of service to God. Even though these beings were angels, God did not overlook their disobedience; He "did not spare them." He punished them by sending them into hell until the time of judgment.

Sent them to hell

The particular word used here for "hell" appears only in 2 Peter 2:4. In classical Greek, this word refers to a subterranean region, doleful and dark, regarded by the ancient Greeks as the abode for the wicked dead. It was thought of as a place of punishment. In this sole New Testament use of the word, it refers to the place of punishment for rebellious angels.

The Flood (v. 5)

Because of the ungodliness of people of the ancient world, God brought a flood that destroyed them. It was a great and awful judgment. Whereas the judgment of the angels is being partly reserved until the end time, the Flood was judgment that came at the time of provocation. To the false teachers Peter was addressing, it is a powerful illustration of the certainty of God's wrath against evil.

Sodom and Gomorrah (v. 6)

God burned to ashes the cities of Sodom and Gomorrah because of their rebellion and immoral behavior. We can see from the account of these cities that it is a terrible thing for rebellious and unrepentant sinners to fall into the hands of a righteous God. Whenever Christians become comfortable in the presence of sin, they are in grave danger of accepting it in others and of embracing it for themselves.

Within these illustrations, we see a lesson. God delivered both Noah and Lot from the judgment that befell their evil worlds.

■ *Peter used three Old Testament examples of*
■ *judgment on sin to show the certainty of pun-*
■ *ishment for followers of false teachers:*
■ *(1) the casting out of fallen angels; (2) the*
■ *Flood; and (3) Sodom and Gomorrah.*

The Destiny of the Disobedient

Illustration	Offending Sin	God's Action	Destiny
Fallen Angels	Rebellion against God	"Did not spare the angels"	Angels sent into hell; will be judged at the end time
People of the Ancient World	Rebellion against God	"Did not spare the ancient world"	Unbelievers destroyed
Cites of Sodom and Gomorrah	Rebellion against God	"Made them an example"	Cities condemned to extinction

THE CHARACTERISTICS OF FALSE TEACHERS (2:10–22)

They Are Arrogant (vv. 10b–11)

These false teachers are so bold as to "slander celestial beings." They recklessly dare to defy God, not hesitating to scoff or scorn the Almighty. Even the more powerful angels do not commit such slander.

They Are Brutes in Their Understanding (v. 12)

False teachers speak evil of matters they do not understand. Peter said that they are like "brute beasts, creatures of instinct, born only to be caught and destroyed" (v. 12). Their end is destruction.

They Are Dominated by Lust and Greed (vv. 13–16)

These deceivers live constantly for luxury and sensuality. Peter called them "blots and blemishes" (v. 13). In verse 14 he listed several telltale activities of their lust and greed:

- Their eyes are "full of adultery."
- They "never stop sinning."
- They "seduce the unstable."
- They are "experts in greed."

Not only are these deceivers unbelieving and immoral, but they are also clearly slaves of their unbelief and victims of their immorality.

They Falsely Claim to Know Jesus (vv. 17–22)

Here Peter warned those who make a superficial commitment to Jesus Christ and turn back are in a more culpable state than before their initial response to Christ. The false teachers had experienced some knowledge of Christian truth that had given them a short victory over worldly corruption. A true knowledge of Jesus would have affected them permanently. However, having turned from the truth about Christ, which they had once believed, they are now in a worse condition. As a result, their willful rejection makes their disobedience a more blameworthy experience.

A real danger here to the Christian community is that the influence of false teachers can tempt Christians to fail in their commitment to Jesus and to "backslide."

In verse 22, Peter used two proverbs to hammer home his point:

To reform one's life without regenerating one's life is futile.

1. "A dog returns to his vomit."
2. "A sow that is washed goes back to her wallowing in the mud."

Those who use their freedom to become again entangled and overpowered by the defilements of sin are like the dog and sow. They never genuinely change.

■ *False teachers are characterized by arro-*
■ *gance, lust, and greed. Although they make a*
■ *pretense of faith, their faith is not genuine.*

QUESTIONS TO GUIDE YOUR STUDY

1. What are false teachers? According to Peter, what is their agenda?
2. What is a "heresy." Why are heresies so potentially destructive?
3. Peter provided three illustrations of the destiny of those who rebel against God. What lessons do we learn from them?
4. What are the characteristics of false teachers? What can believers do to guard against these "brute beasts" (2 Pet. 2:12)?

2 PETER 3

Return of Christ

The New Testament clearly teaches that Jesus will return. His Second Coming will be physical and personal, as were His Resurrection and Ascension (Acts 1:10–11). His coming will be immediately preceded by cosmic and terrestrial distress (Luke 21:25–27). Christ's return will bring upon the world judgment that is sudden, unexpected, and inescapable (Matt. 24:42–44). The Antichrist figure is to arise prior to the Second Coming. He will be decisively overthrown (2 Thess. 2:1–8). The kingdom of God, God's rule and reign, will be fully established at Christ's return.

The theme of this chapter is Christ's return. Here Peter gave his final warnings to the false teachers while providing his readers with encouragement and assurance by reminding them of the certainty of Christ's return.

The fact of Jesus' promised return should spark a new attitude of holiness and commitment in the minds of Jesus' followers. In fact, Peter hinted that Christians can "speed" Jesus' return by renewed vigor in evangelism and devout living.

THE UNRIGHTEOUS AND THE FAITHFUL (3:1–13)

God's Judgment on the Unrighteous (vv. 1–7)

Peter began this section by reminding his readers that this letter to them is his second. He desires that they recall the words of the prophets and "the command given by our Lord and Savior through your apostles."

Raising questions about Jesus' return was one of the ways false teachers were seeking to undermine the faith of Peter's readers. Understanding that the Second Coming was imminent, many early Christians were making the mistake of setting the date of His return during their lifetime.

Peter discouraged date setting, explaining that God's schedule is from a different perspective than ours and much more patiently worked out. In addition, scoffers will come and question Jesus' coming: "Where is this coming he promised?" (v. 4).

Once again, using a triad formula, Peter offers three examples of God's scheduling:

1. Creation (Gen. 1)
2. The Flood (Gen. 6)
3. The final judgment

These three examples refute the scoffer's argument that "everything goes on as it has since the beginning of creation." They show that God indeed has broken into history and, as in the case of the Flood, He did so when men were convinced nothing would befall them.

Heavens will disappear with a roar

The word *roar* is from a Greek word, an adverb that means "with great suddenness," "with a loud noise," or "with a loud roar." Fritz Reinecker's *Linguistic Key to the Greek New Testament* provides this insight: "This word means 'with a hissing or crackling sound.' The word is onomatopoeic, expressing the whizzing sound produced by rapid motion through the air and was used of shrill rushing sounds, the hissing of a snake, the whir of a bird's wings, the hurtling of an arrow and is then used for the rushing movement itself or the accompanying crash or roar. Here probably the roaring of flame is meant" (p. 781).

God's Deliverance for the Faithful (vv. 8–13)

God's plan shows patience (vv. 8–9). Although God accomplishes His purposes by His own timetable, He is "not slow in keeping his promise" (v. 8). Time, although considered a crucial commodity among human beings, is not a great issue with God. Indeed, "with the Lord a day is like a thousand years, and a thousand years are like a day." God will act at precisely the right time to fulfill His promises.

There is a greater plan at work here. Peter emphasized that God's patience leads to salvation for many. He is "not wanting anyone to perish, but everyone to come to repentance" (v. 9).

Christ's return will be sudden (vv. 10–12). Peter believed that Christ's promise to return will be fulfilled with destructive power at a time when sinners will least expect it. It will "come like a thief." Peter described the accompanying destruction with three phases:

1. "The heavens will disappear with a roar."
2. "The elements will be destroyed by fire."
3. "The earth and everything in it will be laid bare."

God will keep His promise (v. 13). But God will deliver the faithful. When He finishes clearing out the old order, He will bring in His new order characterized by righteousness: "But in keeping with his promise we are looking forward to a new heaven and a new earth, the home of righteousness." While waiting for the Lord's return, Christians are to cultivate holiness and godliness in their lives.

The Old Order Versus The New Order

Point of Contrast	Old Order	New Order
Dwelling place:	Fallen world	New heaven and new earth
Characterized by:	Sin	Righteousness

■ *According to His own timetable, God will*
■ *surely send sudden and destructive judgment*
■ *upon the unrighteous. God will keep His*
■ *promise and deliver His faithful to "a new*
■ *heaven and a new earth, the home of righteousness" (v. 13).*

CLOSING COMMANDS (3:14–18a)
Referring to his readers as "dear friends," Peter reminded them that an anticipation of Christ's return carries with it the incentive to maintain and produce a holy life. He referred to Paul's writings as a support for Peter's belief that divine patience was a factor in the delay of Jesus' return. Many see here a reference by Peter to Romans, but Peter leaves his Pauline source unstated.

Be blameless and at peace with God. While awaiting the Lord's return, Christians are to make an effort to maintain the purity of their lives and remain at peace with God. In Romans, we also find that the apostle Paul admonishes believers to "offer your bodies as living sacrifices, holy and pleasing to God" (12:1).

Bear in mind God's patience. Because God is patiently waiting for all people to come to repentance, He has delayed His judgment. Christians need to understand this current period, known as the church age, as a time of continued opportunity for winning others to Christ.

Be on guard. Believers are to keep watch and guard themselves against lawless people and prevent losing their stability. God establishes believers in the faith; but they must constantly be on their guard against false teachers, false doctrines, and false ethics to avoid stumbling.

Grow in grace and knowledge. Peter boldly stated that believers may protect themselves spiritually by mature spiritual growth. This "knowledge" they need is a development in personal acquaintance with Christ.

Grow in grace

The word *grow* means "to advance," or "to increase." It is used of both physical and spiritual growth. Grammatically, the preposition *in* can express two meanings. It can mean: (1) grace as the sphere of one's growth, or (2) grace as the means of one's growth.

- Peter reminded his readers that an anticipation of Christ's return carries with it the incentive to produce a holy life. He then set forth a series of commands intended to encourage his readers to godly living in anticipation of the Lord's return.

CONCLUSION (3:18*b*)

Peter now drew his letter to a close. He covered several key themes:

- living the Christian life
- rejecting the influence of false teachers
- preparing for the Lord's return

In closing, Peter pronounced a simple but beautiful benediction. It is a powerful affirmation of faith and focuses on the person and work of Jesus Christ. "To him be the glory now and forever" is the shout of triumphant faith of all Christians in all ages.

QUESTIONS TO GUIDE YOUR STUDY

1. Why has God delayed Jesus' return?
2. From Peter's words in this chapter, what do we learn about the nature of Christ's return?
3. As Christians anticipate Christ's return, what kind of attitude should it instill in them?
4. As Christians await Christ's return, in what sort of activities should they engage?

Although a brief letter, Jude makes a significant contribution to early Christian literature that calls on believers to defend the faith God has entrusted to the church.

Jude says that his intention was to write about the salvation believers share. However, a situation arose which caused him to address false teaching in the church.

These teachers erred both in their theology and, as a consequence, in their ethics. These teachings had some of the features that appeared in a second century phenomenon called Gnosticism.

One of the key errors of these teachers was that they believed that God's grace implied that there were no moral guidelines.

AUTHOR

The author identified himself as "a servant of Jesus Christ and a brother of James" (v. 2). In presenting himself as a brother of the Lord's half brother (Jas. 1:1), he modestly neglected to mention his own relationship to Jesus (Matt. 13:55; Mark 6:3). Some have identified Jude as "Judas son of James" (Luke 6:16), but the author does not claim apostleship.

DATE OF WRITING

Date. Suggestions for dating this letter vary widely. Little evidence is available for making a conclusive decision. We cannot be certain whether Jude was younger or older than Jesus, but it is likely that he was younger. If Jude were born during the early part of the first century, the letter could have been written about

A.D. 65–80. Because of the uncertainty of the time of its writing, scholars have assigned dates ranging from A.D. 60 to A.D. 140.

AUDIENCE

No address for a reader appears within the letter. The readers might have been Jews or Gentiles who lived anywhere. Jude had a concrete situation in mind, but it is impossible to locate it precisely. The statements of verses 17–18 have led some to suggest that the readers knew apostles within the region of Palestine. This is a possible but unproven hypothesis.

PURPOSE FOR WRITING

Jude intended to produce a message about the common salvation he shared with his readers (v. 3). His awareness of the appearance of heresy led him to change his emphasis to a denunciation of the heresy surrounding him. Jude gave direction for halting the advance of heresy among his readers in verses 17–23.

THEME

Jude began with the intention of discussing the theme of "salvation." Awareness of the infiltration of false teachers led Jude to emphasize two features:

1. He warned against and condemned false teachers who were heavily influencing his area.
2. He urged his readers to greater firmness and commitment.

RELATIONSHIP OF JUDE'S LETTER TO 2 PETER

Most of Jude is included in 2 Peter, but it is an agreement in thought and vocabulary rather than a verbatim reproduction. It is difficult to determine which writer borrowed from the other or whether both used a third, common source. Conclusions reached about this relationship do influence views of authorship and date.

LITERARY FORM

Despite the lack of a specific address, Jude's letter is directed to a specific situation. It is more impersonal than John' epistles. Jude was fond of mentioned items in triads (v. 2: "mercy, peace, and love"; v. 11: Cain, Balaam, and Korah). The majestic doxology provides a moving conclusion to Jude's words (vv. 24–25).

THE THEOLOGY OF JUDE

The epistle contains little theological content because the purpose was largely practical. One controversial feature of the book is the references to the apocryphal books of *First Enoch* (v. 14) and the *Assumption of Moses* (v. 9). Some have seen these references as a liability to accepting the authority of Jude, but Paul quoted a heathen poet in Acts 17:28. He also referred to a noncanonical writing in 2 Timothy 3:8.

Jude appears to have viewed his references to the Apocrypha as authoritative, and he apparently accepted the historicity of the incident in the *Assumption of Moses*. He used his reference more as an illustration to substantiate his points.

BASIC OUTLINE FOR JUDE

Apocrypha

The Apocrypha is a collective term referring to a large body of religious writings dating back to the early Christian centuries. These writings are similar in form to the New Testament but were never included as a part of the canon of Scripture. In the formation of the Christian canon of Scripture, *apocrypha* came to mean works that were not divinely inspired and authoritative.

The Apocrypha is significant for those who study church history. Even though these writings are not included in the Christian canon, they still have value. They give a sample of the ideas, convictions, and imaginations of a portion of Christian history. While the New Testament Apocrypha is often interesting and informative, it is usually unreliable historically and always unauthoritative for matters of faith and practice.

QUESTIONS TO GUIDE YOUR STUDY

1. What was Jude's purpose for writing this letter?
2. Who was his audience? Where were they located?
3. What is the relationship of Jude's letter to 2 Peter?
4. What is Gnosticism? Why did Jude react so strongly to its presence in the Christian community?

JUDE

The force (tense) of the verbs "loved" and "kept" emphasize God's continuing love and protection. Believers of Jesus today may also take comfort in Jude's greeting to his brothers and sisters in Christ, knowing that God exercises the same love and protection for us.

SALUTATION (1–2)

Jude identified himself as a follower of Christ and "a brother of James" (v. 2). Jude is listed among the brothers of Jesus (Mark 6:3). His brother James gave no geographical designation to his readers, but he presented them as those who were "called," "loved by God," and "kept by Jesus Christ." This threefold wish is an example of Jude's affinity for triads, groupings of threes.

Characteristics of Jude's Readers in verse 2

READER CHARACTERISTIC	EXPLANATION
"Called"	Those who had accepted the invitation to become disciples of Jesus
"Loved by God"	Divine love that always includes positive goodwill towards its object
"Kept by Jesus Christ"	Jesus keeps a watchful care over them and protects them from harm

Jude wished his readers an experience of mercy that would allow them to know the benefits of love and peace. By using the word "abundance," Jude was wishing that they might see mercy, love, and peace increase in their Christian experience.

- *Jude's greeting is a wish of God's love and*
- *protection upon his readers as well as a*
- *desire to see God's love and peace multiply in*
- *their lives.*

A PLEA FOR SOUND DOCTRINE (3–4)

A Shared Salvation (v. 3)

Most scholars agree that Jude originally prepared to write a letter about the mutual body of Christian teachings ("the salvation we share") but diverted his attention toward a growing heresy because of its imminent threat to the faith of is readers.

A Defense for the Faith (v. 3)

When Jude learned of the presence of heretics among them who denied Christ, he urged his friends into a continuous, vigorous defense of the faith: "contend for the faith" (v .3). The word translated *contend* or *struggle* is used only here in the New Testament. This verb expresses the kind of intensity seen in wrestlers. This contention for the faith is not a one time action but is continuous.

The faith is that body of truth that came to be recognized as the essentials of Christianity.

Contending for the faith involves (1) defending the faith against threat or attack, and (2) living godly, obedient lives to resist heresy.

The Problem Group (v. 4)

Apparently, a group has "secretly slipped" into the Christian community. Jude described this group as "godless men" who stood condemned before God because of their denial of Jesus' lordship. These men had crept in secretly, were

Faith

Although the term *faith* usually means a personal commitment in the Bible, here it has the definite article ("the") and clearly seems to refer to a body of Christian teachings or doctrines. That this faith "was once for all entrusted to the saints" further underscores that Jude was referring to an established body of teachings.

teaching false doctrines, and were living in sin. There are two likely ways these men were denying Christ:

1. By rejecting His deity.
2. By living sinful lives contrary to Jesus' teaching (see 2 Pet. 2:1).

■ *The salvation the believers possessed was a*
■ *common salvation; that is, one they shared.*
■ *Jude urged his readers to defend the faith vig-*
■ *orously, the body of teachings that had been*
■ *entrusted to them.*

A WARNING AGAINST FALSE DOCTRINE (5–16)

A Lesson from History (vv. 5–7)

The teaching about God's grace and forgiveness has been distorted repeatedly from the very beginning to imply that we can do anything we want and still be God's people.

The tendency to sentimentalize God's love in the last two centuries has come from a neglect of the Old Testament and a reading of the New Testament selectively.

Here Jude cites three cases of God's judgment in history. These cases show God's eternal opposition to evil:

1. The judgment of God in the wilderness (Num. 32:10–13).

God had graciously delivered His people from slavery in Egypt. He provided food and water for them daily on their journey from Egypt to Canaan. He protected them from their enemies in miraculous ways. His intention was to give

Contend

The word for *contend* is a compound word made up of two words: (1) a preposition that means "upon" or "about," attached to (2) a verb that means "to contest." The attached preposition serves to intensify the verb. In some translations, the word *earnestly* is added to convey the intensive force of the preposition.

Therefore, *contend* means "to struggle for, to contend for, to exercise great effort and exertion for something." It was often used of those who participated in athletic contests, describing their struggles and efforts to win the prize. [See *Vine's Complete Expository Dictionary of Old and New Testament Words* (Nashville: Thomas Nelson, 1996), 125.]

them and their children a rich inheritance in the land he promised to Abraham.

And yet, almost all of Israel rebelled against God. As a consequence, His anger burned against them and He determined that only Joshua and Caleb would enter the Promised Land. He allowed the rest to wander in the wilderness for forty years and die.

2. The angels who lost their positions of authority because they disobeyed God. As a result, they have been imprisoned until the day of judgment. The likely reference here is Genesis 6:4 as interpreted in the Book of Enoch.

3. The destruction of Sodom and Gomorrah (Gen. 19:24–29).

The sins of these cities were so great that God destroyed them—sparing only Lot and his family.

These three instances show God's strong aversion to sin. Jude implies that God hasn't changed—that He is still opposed to sin.

A Description of the False Teachers (vv. 8–13)

Jude characterizes the false teachers as dreamers which could refer to their relying on dreams as a source of their teaching, or they could be so out of touch with reality that they were characterized as dreamers.

He charges them with defiling their bodies, rebelling against authority, and making fun of angels. Apparently they were so focussed on the flesh that they talked glibly about spiritual realities, the existence of which they may have doubted.

Examples from the Old Testament. Here Jude used historical examples from the Old Testament to characterize the false teachers as materialistic and immoral. These characteristics include:

- Unreasoning animals
- Shepherds who feed only themselves
- Clouds without rain
- Barren trees, without fruit and uprooted
- Wild waves of the sea that wash up refuse
- Wandering stars for whom blackest darkness has been reserved

Jude charged the false teachers with leading others astray. He then referred to some well-known examples of Old Testament deceivers who led many astray: Cain, Balaam, and Korah.

"'Wandering stars' referred to the erratic orbits of planets, sometimes attributed to disobedient angels, who were to be imprisoned under God's judgement and are called 'stars' in 1 Enoch." [*The IVP Bible Background Commentary, New Testament* (Downers Grove: InterVarsity Press, 1993), 755.]

Old Testament Deceivers' "Hall of Shame"

CHARACTER	SIN
Cain	"The way of Cain"; rejected God's revelation and refused to make a blood sacrifice; worshiped God his own way
Balaam	Greed; led others into sins for personal gain
Korah	Rebelliousness; rejected the authority of Moses and tried to assume power for himself

A Picture from 1 Enoch. Jude cited a statement, a picture of judgment, from 1 Enoch 1:9 to prove the reality of divine judgment upon the ungodly. It speaks of the eventual judgment of wicked people like false teachers. Jesus made a similar statement when He said, "When the Son of Man comes in his glory, and all the angels with him" (Matt. 25:31). Jude is not necessarily viewing 1 Enoch as inspired Scripture, but he is referring to a book his readers would know and respect.

Concluding Remarks. Jude closed this section by making a final characterization of the false teachers.. The characteristics he chose to describe them include:

- Grumblers
- Faultfinders
- Lustful
- Boastful
- Flatterers

■ *Jude issued warnings to the false teachers.*
■ *He drew examples from history, the Old Tes-*
■ *tament, and extrabiblical literature to*
■ *expose the evil characteristics of these here-*
■ *tics. God will hold these evil men account-*
■ *able for their actions.*

ENCOURAGEMENT TO FAITHFULNESS (17–23)

Contending for the Faith Through Argument (vv. 17–19)

Jude reminded his readers "what the apostles of our Lord Jesus Christ foretold" (v. 17). This body of apostolic writings included "predictions" that "in the last times there will be scoffers who will follow their own ungodly desires" (v. 18). The scoffers would come, bringing their divisiveness and spiritual emptiness. Likely, Jude was referring to such general warnings as Acts 20:29–30 and 1 Timothy

4:1–3 to show that the apostles foretold the coming of these men.

Contending for the Faith Through Spiritual Growth (vv. 20–23)

Jude wanted his readers to build up themselves with prayer and obedience. He urged his readers to practice five disciplines that would prepare them to resist the false teachers who had infiltrated their community:

1. To build up themselves in their knowledge of God's truth.
2. To pray fervently.
3. To live in the sphere of God's love by obeying His commands.
4. To fan the flames of Christian hope.
5. To practice evangelism and pastoral care with those who might be enticed into following false teachings.

- ■ *Jude wanted his readers to remain faithful to*
- ■ *God. They were to contend for the faith by*
- ■ *remembering what the apostles foretold and*
- ■ *by growing spiritually, practicing several*
- ■ *disciplines Jude set forth.*

DOXOLOGY (24–25)

Jude closed his letter with an unusually beautiful and meaningful doxology. His mind focused on the power of almighty God, who alone provides the strength for full obedience.

In verse 24 he praised God for His sustaining power toward believers. "To him who is able to keep you from falling" refers to God who is able to keep believers from yielding to temptation, whether or not it relates to false teaching.

"This conclusion of the epistle of Jude is grand and soul-stirring. It lifts the thoughts from earthly conflicts with which the author has been compelled to busy himself, up to the heavenly realms, where God is enthroned amidst eternal might and honor. The fight against evil forces in this narrow and dark world should always be viewed in such a luminous cosmic perspective." [Bo Reike from *The Anchor Bible: The Epistles of James, Peter, and Jude* (Garden City: Doubleday & Co., Inc, 1964), 217.]

In verse 25 he ascribed "glory, majesty, power, and authority" to God because of the work of Jesus Christ. Although Jude devoted a good deal of his letter to false teachers and the works of darkness, he concluded by focusing his letter on the attributes of God.

QUESTIONS TO GUIDE YOUR STUDY

1. What is the best way to "contend" for Christian truth? (See also John 13:34–35; 14:21.)

2. What are some of the characteristics of false teachers Jude mentioned in verses 5–16? How common are these traits today?

3. Drawing from the content of his letter, what did Jude's readers have in common with believers today?

4. What are some of the truths about God that we see in Jude's doxology in verses 24–25?

The following list is a collection of the works used for this volume. All are from Broadman & Holman's list of published reference resources. They will accommodate the reader's need for more specific information and for an expanded treatment of 1, 2 Peter, Jude. All of these works will greatly aid in the reader's study, teaching, and presentation of 1, 2 Peter, Jude. The accompanying annotations can be helpful in guiding the reader to the proper resources.

Adams, J. McKee. Rev. by Joseph A. Callaway. *Biblical Backgrounds*. This work provides valuable information on the physical and geographical settings of the New Testament. Its many colorful maps and other features add depth and understanding.

Blair, Joe. *Introducing the New Testament*, 197–204. Designed as a core text for New Testament survey courses, this volume helps the reader in understanding the content and principles of the New Testament. Its features include, maps and photos, outlines, and discussion questions.

Cate, Robert L., *A History of the New Testament and Its Times*. An excellent and thorough survey of the birth and growth of the Christian faith in the first-century world.

Holman Bible Dictionary. An exhaustive, alphabetically arranged resource of Bible-related subjects. An excellent tool of definitions and other information on people, places, things, and events.

Holman Bible Handbook, 762–70, 781–82. A comprehensive treatment that offers outlines, commentary on key themes and sections, and full-color photos, illustrations, charts, and maps. Provides an accent on broader theological teachings.

Howard, Fred D. *1, 2, 3 John, Jude, Revelation,* Layman's Bible Book Commentary, vol. 24, 43–49. A popular-level treatment of several of Paul's epistles, including Jude. This easy-to-use volume provides a relevant and practical perspective for the reader.

Lea, Thomas D. *The New Testament: Its Background and Message,* 533–57, 575–83. An excellent resource for background material—political, cultural, historical, and religious. Provides background information in both broad strokes on specific books, including the Gospels.

McQuay, Earl P. *Keys to Interpreting the Bible.* This work provides a fine introduction to the study of the Bible that is invaluable for home Bible studies, lay members of a local church, or students.

McQuay, Earl P., *Learning to Study the Bible.* This study guide presents a helpful procedure that employs the principles basic to effective and thorough Bible study. Using Philippians as a model, the various methods of Bible study are applied. Excellent for home Bible studies, lay members of a local church, and students.

Robertson, A. T., *A Grammar of the Greek New Testament in the Light of Historical Research.* An exhaustive, scholarly work on the underlying language of the New Testament. Provides advanced insights into the grammatical, syntactical, and lexical aspects of the New Testament.

Valentine, Foy. *Hebrews, James, 1, 2 Peter,* Layman's Bible Book Commentary, vol. 23, 43–49. A popular treatment of several epistles, including 1, 2 Peter. This easy-to-use volume provides a relevant and practical perspective for the reader.

SHEPHERD'S
NOTES

SHEPHERD'S NOTES

SHEPHERD'S NOTES